# Punny or Not
# Book of Puns

Copyright © 2020 by Yowza Publishing


Published by Yowza Publishing
YowzaPublishing.com


ISBN: 978-1-951410-04-9
Version 1.0.0
Printing: 10 9 8 7 6 5 4 3 2 1

Cover Image by Shanon from Pixabay

All rights reserved. No part of this publication may be reproduced, stored in a retrieval system, or transmitted in any form or by any means without prior written permission of the publisher. The only exception is brief quotations in printed reviews.

# Punny or Not
# Book of Puns

Bradley Jones

As you read this book, remember….

Seven days without a pun makes one weak.

# Punny or Not Book of Puns

## Table of Contents

| | |
|---|---|
| Animal Puns | 1 |
| Cat Puns | 15 |
| Dog Puns | 23 |
| Fantasy Puns | 29 |
| Food Puns | 31 |
| Punny People | 45 |
| Pun with the Wife | 63 |
| Math Puns | 65 |
| Pun at School | 69 |
| Science Puns | 73 |
| Out of This World (Space) Puns | 79 |
| Sports Puns | 83 |
| Puns Around the House | 87 |
| Pun with Dates and Time | 95 |
| Language Puns | 97 |
| Puns Like No Others (Miscellaneous) | 99 |

## Animal Puns

WHAT'S THE DIFFERENCE BETWEEN A HIPPO AND A ZIPPO? ONE IS REALLY HEAVY AND THE OTHER IS A LITTLE LIGHTER!

~ ~ ~

What did the duck say when she purchased new lipstick?
Put it on my bill!

~ ~ ~

*Who is a penguin's favorite aunt?*
*Aunt-Arctica!*

~ ~ ~

*I once met a pig that did karate; We called him Pork Chop!*

~ ~ ~

A police officer told me my dog was changing people on bikes. That's ridiculous!
My dog doesn't even own a bike!

~ ~ ~

**What is the musical part of a snake?**
**The scales!**

~ ~ ~

Why was the baby ant confused?
Because all his uncles were ants!

~ ~ ~

What do you call a thieving alligator?
A Crookodile!

~ ~ ~

What do you call a bee that can't make up its mind? A Maybe.

~ ~ ~

**What do you call a pig that does karate? Pork chop!**

~ ~ ~

Two birds are sitting on a perch and one says, "Do you smell fish?"

~ ~ ~

What do you call a cow with no legs?
Ground beef.

~ ~ ~

What do you call a cow with two legs?
Lean beef.

~ ~ ~

*What do you call a cow with all its legs?*
*High steaks.*

~ ~ ~

What do you call a bear with no teeth?
A gummy bear.

~ ~ ~

**What's a rabbit's favorite car?**
**Any make as long as it's a hutchback!**

~ ~ ~

What is horse sense? Stable thinking and the ability to say nay!

~ ~ ~

When should you buy a bird?
When it's going cheep!

~ ~ ~

Why do cows wear bells?
Because their horns don't work

~ ~ ~

*What's the difference between deer nuts and beer nuts?*
*Beer nuts are $3.75, whereas deer nuts are under a buck.*

~ ~ ~

A friend tried to annoy me with bird puns.
I soon realized that toucan play at that game.

~ ~ ~

# Why couldn't the leopard play hide and seek? Because he was always spotted.

~ ~ ~

Why do seagulls fly over the sea? Because if they flew over the bay, they'd be bagels!

~ ~ ~

A TERMITE WALKS INTO A BAR AND SAYS, "WHERE IS THE BAR TENDER?"

~ ~ ~

I don't like insect puns. They bug me.

~ ~ ~

Why did the bee get married?
Because he found his honey.

~ ~ ~

*Why was the horse so happy? Because he lived in a stable environment.*

~ ~ ~

Why don't oysters share their pearls?
Because they're shellfish.

~ ~ ~

Did you hear about the 2 silkworms in a race?
It ended in a tie.

~ ~ ~

Why did the lion break up with his girlfriend?
Because she was a cheetah!

~ ~ ~

**Why did the Easter egg hide? Because it was a little chicken!**

~ ~ ~

*Why did the octopus beat the shark in a fight? Because the octopus was well armed.*

~ ~ ~

Pay no attention to the elephant in the room; it is ir-elephant.

~ ~ ~

**Cows lie down in the rain to keep each udder dry.**

~ ~ ~

*What is the best way to communicate with a fish?*
*Drop it a line.*

~ ~ ~

WHAT DO YOU CALL AN OWL THAT DOES MAGIC TRICKS?
HOODINI.

~ ~ ~

*What did the mother lion say to her cubs before dinner? "Shall we prey!"*

~ ~ ~

What did the buffalo say to his son when he dropped him off at school?

Bison.

~ ~ ~

WHICH BEAR IS THE MOST CONDESCENDING?
A PAN-DUH!

~ ~ ~

Why did the prawn leave the nightclub?
Because he pulled a muscle.

~ ~ ~

**Why did the pig stop sunbathing? He was bacon in the heat.**

~ ~ ~

*I went geese hunting the other day, but once they started flying, I knew the game was up.*

~ ~ ~

# How does a penguin build his house?
# Igloos it together.

There's nothing punny about a blank page.

## Cat Puns

*What kind of sports car does a cat drive?*
*A Furrari!*

~ ~ ~

What do you call it when a cat wins a dog show?
A cat-ha-trophy!

~ ~ ~

**What is a cat's favorite college course?**
**Mewsic theory!**

~ ~ ~

*What did the cat say when his friend didn't believe him?*
*"Listen, I'm fur real!"*

~ ~ ~

WHAT DO YOU CALL A CAT THAT CONVINCES YOU TO GIVE IT WHAT IT WANTS?
PURRSUASIVE!

~ ~ ~

What do you call a cat caught by the police?
A purrpatrator!

~ ~ ~

What do you call a cat and dog
that really like each other?
Best furends!

~ ~ ~

How is your cat doing today?
She's feline fine!

~ ~ ~

**What was the mean cat's favorite subject in school? Hissstory!**

~ ~ ~

What's a cat's most important trait?
It's purrsonality!

~ ~ ~

*What did the cat draw in art class?*
*A self pawtrait!*

~ ~ ~

What do cats wear to sleep in?
Pawjamas!

~ ~ ~

Why are there no cats on Mar?
Curiosity killed the cat!

~ ~ ~

WHY DIDN'T THE CAT GO TO THE VET?
HE WAS FELINE FINE!

~ ~ ~

Did you hear about the cat that
swallowed a ball of yarn?
She gave birth to an entire
litter of mittens.

~ ~ ~

What is it called when a cat paints itself?
A self paw-trait.

~ ~ ~

**Why don't cats like shopping online?
They prefer cat-alogues!**

~ ~ ~

*What do you call a pile of kittens?*
*A meowntain.*

~ ~ ~

What do you call a cat that can't stop licking itself?
Purrr-verted.

~ ~ ~

WHAT DO YOU GET WHEN YOU CROSS A CAT WITH FATHER CHRISTMAS?
SANTA CLAWS!

~ ~ ~

*What is a cat's favorite color?*
*Purrrple!*

~ ~ ~

There are a dozen cats on a ledge. One jumps off. How many are left?
None, because they were all a bunch of copycats!

~ ~ ~

What do you call a cat that likes to read?
Litter-ate.

~ ~ ~

Where do you find a birthday present for a cat?
In a cat-alogue!

~ ~ ~

# Punny or Not

There's nothing punny about a blank page.

## Dog Puns

Why do dog's make terrible dancers?
Because they have two left feet!

~ ~ ~

**How do dog catchers get paid?
By the pound!**

~ ~ ~

What do you call a sad puppy?
A mellon collie.

~ ~ ~

What was the dog's favorite type of homework to do?
A lab report!

~ ~ ~

What do you call a dog that can do magic?
A Labracadabrador.

~ ~ ~

Dogs can't operate MRI machines.
But catscan.

~ ~ ~

THE RACE DOG THAT CAME DOWN WITH A BAD CASE OF FLEAS WAS EVENTUALLY SCRATCHED.

~ ~ ~

In order to see the real potential in my dog, there is no begging involved. You simply have to unleash it.

~ ~ ~

The young lady was very upset that her dog swallowed her engagement ring because how she has a diamond in the ruff.

~ ~ ~

*A dog wears its coat in the winter, but as summer approaches it wear its coat and pants.*

~ ~ ~

**The dog that gave birth to puppies at the roadside was eventually ticketed for littering.**

~ ~ ~

THE COACH ALWAYS WANTS TO PUT MY DOG IN THE BASEBALL GAME BECAUSE HE ALWAYS GETS WALKED.

~ ~ ~

The reason that police dogs are so great at their jobs is because of the in-scent-ive.

~ ~ ~

**MY GOLDEN RETRIEVER'S DOG TAG IS OFTEN MISTAKEN FOR COLLAR ID.**

~ ~ ~

Food for very bad dogs is often bought by the pound.

~ ~ ~

*You should always extra careful after it rains cats and dogs. You really don't want to accidentally step in a poodle.*

# Punny or Not

There's nothing punny about a blank page.

## Fantasy Puns

**Why is Cinderella so bad at soccer?
Because she always run away from the ball!**

~ ~ ~

Why is Peter Pan flying all the time?
He Neverlands!

~ ~ ~

*What did Cinderella say when her photos did not show up?
Someday my prints will come!*

~ ~ ~

*Why was Cinderella banned from playing sports?*
*Because she ran away from the ball.*

~ ~ ~

How did the soggy Easter Bunny dry himself?
With a hare dryer!

~ ~ ~

## Food Puns

Why was the cookie sad? Because his mom was a wafer long.

~ ~ ~

**What did the sushi say to the bee?
Wasabee!**

~ ~ ~

My girlfriend thought I'd never be able to make a car out of spaghetti….
You should've seen her face when I drove pasta!

~ ~ ~

Coffee has a rough time in our house. It gets mugged every single morning!

~ ~ ~

My parent said I can't drink coffee anymore, or else they'll ground me!

~ ~ ~

What did the mayonnaise say when somebody opened the refrigerator?
"Hey, close the door! I'm dressing!"

~ ~ ~

**Time flies like an arrow. Fruit flies like a banana!**

~ ~ ~

*How do you make a good egg-roll?*
*You push it down a hill!*

~ ~ ~

Why do eggs hate jokes?
The answers crack them up!

~ ~ ~

**I became a vegetarian.
Huge missed-steak!**

~ ~ ~

What do you call an average potato?
A commen-tator!

~ ~ ~

How does Moses make coffee?
Hebrews it.

~ ~ ~

Did you hear about the guy that was hit in the head with a can of soda?
He was lucky it was a soft drink!

~ ~ ~

WHAT KIND OF DOCTOR IS DR. PEPPER?
A FIZZ-ICIAN!

~ ~ ~

What do you call a beautiful pumpkin?
Gourd-geous!

~ ~ ~

Why did one banana spy on the other?
Because she was appealing.

~ ~ ~

## Sausage puns are the wurst.

~ ~ ~

What happens when you eat too many spaghetti-o's?
You have a vowel movement.

~ ~ ~

There was a fight in the candy store.
Two suckers got licked.

~ ~ ~

*Winning candy as a prize is always a sweet victory!*

~ ~ ~

The cook's ability to find fresh vegetables on sale was uncanny!

~ ~ ~

I'VE JUST WRITTEN A SONG ABOUT TORTILLAS.
ACTUALLY, IT'S MORE OF A RAP.

~ ~ ~

*My first job was working in an orange juice factory, but I got canned - couldn't concentrate.*

~ ~ ~

I ordered 2000 pounds of Chinese soup.
It was Won Ton.

~ ~ ~

Cannibals like to meat people.

~ ~ ~

If you believe that the quickest way to a man's heart is the stomach, then you are aiming a little too high.

~ ~ ~

What do ghosts serve for dessert?
I scream.

~ ~ ~

I HAD A JOB TYING SAUSAGES TOGETHER, BUT I COULDN'T MAKE ENDS MEET.

~ ~ ~

Why don't cannibals eat clowns?
They taste funny.

~ ~ ~

*A vegan said, "People who sell meat are gross!" I responded, "People who sell fruits and vegetable are grocer."*

~ ~ ~

# I was going to share a vegetable joke, but it was corny.

~ ~ ~

What do you call a fake noodle?
An impasta!

~ ~ ~

A cheese truck crashed.
De brie was everywhere.

~ ~ ~

Nobody ever asks how Coca-Cola is doing.
It's always, "Is Pepsi okay?"

~ ~ ~

**Went to quite a few stores to find the best prices for herbs.
It was thyme well spent.**

~ ~ ~

I need to stop drinking milk.
It is an udder disgrace.

~ ~ ~

WHERE DID THE SPAGHETTI AND THE SAUCE GO DANCING?
THE MEATBALL!

~ ~ ~

Did you hear about the pessimist who hates German sausage?
He always fears the Wurst.

~ ~ ~

*I asked my friend a question while he was eating an orange, but all I got was a pithy response.*

~ ~ ~

Last night I dreamed I was swimming in an ocean of orange soda, but it was just a Fanta sea.

~ ~ ~

I could tell a joke about pizza, but it is a little cheesy.

~ ~ ~

A slice of apple pie is $3.00 in Jamaica and $3.50 in the Bahamas.
These are the pie rates of the Caribbean.

~ ~ ~

**Did you hear the rumor about the butter? Well, I'm not going to spread it!**

~ ~ ~

I accidentally swallowed some food coloring.
The doctor says I'm okay, but I feel like I've dyed a little inside.

~ ~ ~

Have you ever tried to eat a clock?
It's very time consuming.

~ ~ ~

*My friend's bakery burned down last night.*
*Now his business is toast.*

~ ~ ~

It was an emotional wedding.
Even the cake was in tiers.

~ ~ ~

A BOILED EGG IN THE MORNING IS HARD TO BEAT.

~ ~ ~

This page is no pun! It looks empty, but it's not....

## Punny People

**I asked a Frenchman if he played video games. He said Wii!**

~ ~ ~

Three conspiracy theorists walk into a bar. You can't tell me that's just a coincidence!

~ ~ ~

I have a few jokes about unemployed people, but none of them work!

~ ~ ~

What do you call an overweight psychic? A four-chin teller!

~ ~ ~

DID YOU HEAR ABOUT THE GUY WHO HAD HIS LEFT LEG AND LEFT ARM AMPUTATED? HE'S ALL RIGHT NOW!

~ ~ ~

I bought some shoes from a drug dealer. I don't know what they are laced with, but I've been tripping all day!

~ ~ ~

*Why did the diet coach send her clients to the paint store?*

*They heard you could get thinner there.*

~ ~ ~

Did you hear about the young actor who fell through the floorboards?
He was just going through a stage!

~ ~ ~

*A scarecrow says, "This job isn't for everybody, but hay, it's in my jeans."*

~ ~ ~

The soldier who survived mustard gas and pepper spray was a seasoned veteran.

~ ~ ~

**Claustrophobic people are more productive thinking out of the box.**

~ ~ ~

A Mexican magician was doing a magic trick. He said, "Uno, Dose," and then he disappeared without a trace!

~ ~ ~

*"Doctor, there's a patient on line 1 that says he is invisible." "Well, tell him I can't see him right now."*

~ ~ ~

Atheists don't solve exponential equations because they don't believe in higher powers.

~ ~ ~

If a child refuses to sleep during nap time, are they guilty of resisting a rest?

~ ~ ~

*Most people are shocked when they find out how incompetent I am as an electrician.*

~ ~ ~

**The boss is going to fire the employee with the worst posture.
I have a hunch; it might be me.**

~ ~ ~

If a short psychic broke out of jail, then you'd have a small medium at large.

~ ~ ~

I WAS GOING TO BE A BANKER, BUT I LOST INTEREST.

~ ~ ~

Police have arrested the world tongue-twister champion. He will probably be given a tough sentence.

~ ~ ~

What is Mozart doing right now? Decomposing.

~ ~ ~

*I worked in the woods as a lumberjack, but I just couldn't hack it, so they gave me the ax.*

~ ~ ~

MY GIRLFRIEND WORKS AT A ZOO. I THINK SHE IS A KEEPER.

~ ~ ~

This morning a clown opened the door for me. I thought to myself, that's a nice Jester.

~ ~ ~

SOMEONE STOLE MY TOILET, AND THE POLICE HAVE NOTHING TO GO ON.

~ ~ ~

I threw an Asian man down a flight of stairs. It was Wong on so many levels.

~ ~ ~

When I was young, I always felt like a male trapped in a female's body. Then I was born.

~ ~ ~

It's hard to explain puns to kleptomaniacs because they always take things literally.

~ ~ ~

*Fishermen are reel men.*

~ ~ ~

## What do you call a priest that becomes a lawyer? A father in law.

~ ~ ~

WHY CAN'T FISHERMEN BE GENEROUS? BECAUSE THEIR BUSINESS MAKES THEM SELL FISH!

~ ~ ~

Two guys walk into a bar. The third one ducks.

~ ~ ~

*How did Ben Franklin feel about discovering electricity? He was shocked!*

~ ~ ~

I lost my job as a stage designer. I wasn't very happy but left without making a scene.

~ ~ ~

Why did the can crusher quit its job? Because it was soda pressing.

~ ~ ~

*I was at a climbing center the other day, but someone had stolen all the grip; honestly, you couldn't make it up.*

~ ~ ~

WHAT DID SPARTACUS DO TO THE CANNIBAL WHO ATE HIS NAGGING WIFE? NOTHING, HE'S GLADIATOR.

~ ~ ~

The fattest knight at King Arthur's round table was Sir Cumference. He acquired his size from too much pi.

~ ~ ~

Why did the invisible man turn down the job offer? Because he couldn't see himself doing it.

~ ~ ~

**Why wasn't the woman happy with the Velcro she bought? It was a total rip-off.**

~ ~ ~

It is easy to get ladies to not eat Tide pods. It's more difficult to deter gents, though.

~ ~ ~

Did you hear about the guy who invented Lifesavers? They say he made a mint.

~ ~ ~

**WHY CAN'T YOU HEAR A PSYCHIATRIST USING THE BATHROOM? BECAUSE THE 'P' IS SILENT.**

~ ~ ~

*When does a joke become a dad joke? When it becomes apparent.*

~ ~ ~

How do you get a country girl's attention? A tractor.

~ ~ ~

What do you call a pudgy psychic? A four-chin teller.

~ ~ ~

What kind of music do chiropractor's like? Hip pop.

~ ~ ~

*If you need an ark, I Noah guy.*

~ ~ ~

**I used to be a baby, but I grew out of it.**

~ ~ ~

My roommates are concerned that I'm using their kitchen utensils, but that's a whisk I'm willing to take.

~ ~ ~

A criminal's best asset is his lie ability.

~ ~ ~

AMERICANS PREFER HOUSES WITH BASEMENTS. IN FACT, THEY'RE BEST CELLARS!

~ ~ ~

If you've been thinking about singing karaoke with a friend, just duet!

~ ~ ~

*A butcher walked backwards into the meat grinder and got a little behind in his work.*

~ ~ ~

Baby puns are childish, but great puns are full groan.

~ ~ ~

# What's a prisoner's favorite punctuation mark? A period; it marks the end of his sentence.

~ ~ ~

A friend said they didn't understand cloning. I told them that makes two of us.

~ ~ ~

Don't be mad at lazy people, they didn't do anything.

~ ~ ~

There's nothing punny about a blank page.

## Pun with the Wife

*My ex-wife still misses me. Her aim is starting to improve!*

~ ~ ~

**What do you call the wife of a hippie? Mississippi!**

~ ~ ~

My wife refused to go to a nude beach with me. I think she's just being clothes-minded!

~ ~ ~

MY WIFE COOKS FOR ME LIKE I'M A GOD. SHE PLACES BURNT OFFERINGS BEFORE ME EVERY NIGHT.

~ ~ ~

I accidentally handed my wife a glue stik instead of a Chapstick.
She still isn't talking to me.

~ ~ ~

I told my wife it was her time to shovel and salt the front steps. All I got was icy stares.

~ ~ ~

## Math Puns

You really shouldn't be intimidated by advanced math... It's as easy as Pi!

~ ~ ~

**What do you call friends who love math? Algebros!**

~ ~ ~

An opinion without 3.14159 is just an onion

~ ~ ~

*Which Halloween monster is best at math? Count Dracula!*

~ ~ ~

**WHAT DID ONE MATH BOOK SAY TO THE OTHER? DON'T' BOTHER ME, I'VE GOT MY OWN PROBLEMS**

~ ~ ~

I always pray before my trigonometry tests.
I hope for a sine from above!

~ ~ ~

Something about subtraction just doesn't add up.

~ ~ ~

*My math teacher called me average. How mean!*

~ ~ ~

Did you hear about the math teacher who's afraid of negative numbers? He will stop at nothing to avoid them.

~ ~ ~

**Not all math puns are terrible. Just sum.**

~ ~ ~

Why did the girl wear glasses in math class? It improves di-vision.

~ ~ ~

A rubber band slingshot was confiscated in algebra class for being a weapon of math disruption.

~ ~ ~

*There are 10 different kinds of people in the world. The ones who understand binary, and the ones who do not.*

~ ~ ~

**Atheists don't solve exponential equations because they don't believe in higher powers.**

~ ~ ~

## Pun at School

Did you hear about the kidnapping at the school?
It's okay. He woke up!

~ ~ ~

**Never trust math teachers who use graph paper. They are always plotting something!**

~ ~ ~

What's the best place to grow flowers in a school?
In the kindergarten.

~ ~ ~

**A teacher asks a student, "Are you ignorant or just apathetic?" The kid responded, "I don't know, and I don't care."**

~ ~ ~

Teachers who take class attendance are absent-minded

~ ~ ~

DO YOU KNOW WHY THERE AREN'T ANY GOOD SCIENCE PUNS NOWADAYS?
BECAUSE ALL THE GOOD ONES ARGON.

~ ~ ~

*Why are bad school grades like a shipwreck in the ocean? They're both below C level!*

~ ~ ~

## What's the king of all school supplies? The Ruler!

~ ~ ~

A cross eyed teacher couldn't control his pupils.

There's nothing punny about a blank page.

## Science Puns

I'm reading a book about anti-gravity. It's impossible to put down!

~ ~ ~

*What do you do with chemists that die? Barium!*

~ ~ ~

I'D TELL YOU A CHEMISTRY JOKE, BUT I KNOW I WOULDN'T GET A REACTION!

~ ~ ~

# Why did the scientist install a knocker on his front door?
# He wanted to win a No-bell prize!

~ ~ ~

Why shouldn't you trust atoms?
They make up everything.

~ ~ ~

*I was going to make a joke about sodium, but Na...*

~ ~ ~

Iron man is a guy, but he could have been Fe male.

~ ~ ~

Why are atoms Catholic?
Because they have mass.

~ ~ ~

No matter how popular they get, antibiotics will never go viral.

~ ~ ~

**Two blood cells met and fell in love, but alas, it was all in vein.**

~ ~ ~

WHY DO ENZYMES MAKE THE BEST DEEJAYS?
BECAUSE THEY ALWAYS BREAK IT DOWN!

~ ~ ~

*Why isn't energy made of atoms?*
*It doesn't matter.*

~ ~ ~

A photon checks into a hotel and is asked if he needs help with the luggage. He says, "No, I'm traveling light."

~ ~ ~

Seems like I remember my science teacher talking about Pavlov, but it just doesn't ring a bell.

~ ~ ~

My science teacher had a new theory on inertia, but it isn't gaining any momentum.

~ ~ ~

The neutron was always seen hanging out at the local bar because he was never charged.

~ ~ ~

The limestone was overheard telling the geologist not to take him for granite.

~ ~ ~

*Ben Franklin was shocked after he discovered electricity.*

~ ~ ~

All scientists freshen their breath using experi-mints.

~ ~ ~

*Cells multiply by dividing.*

~ ~ ~

## Out of This World (Space) Puns

WHAT DO YOU HAVE TO DO TO HAVE A PARTY IN SPACE?
YOU HAVE TO PLANET.

~ ~ ~

*Why don't aliens visit our planet?*
*Terrible ratings - just one star.*

~ ~ ~

I wanted to be an astronaut, but my parents told me the sky was the limit.

~ ~ ~

How do you get a baby astronaut to go to sleep?
Rocket

~ ~ ~

## Why did the Sun go to school?
## To get brighter!

~ ~ ~

If athletes get "Athletes foot", what can astronauts get?
Missile Toe.

~ ~ ~

## Where do astronauts park their vehicles? At parking Meteors

~ ~ ~

What hot drink do space people like?
Gravi-tea

~ ~ ~

I WAS UP ALL NIGHT WONDERING WHERE THE SUN HAD GONE, BUT THEN IT FINALLY DAWNED ON ME!

~ ~ ~

Every time I see a picture of something amazing in space, I usually say "that's totally far out."

~ ~ ~

Why did the Sun never go to college?
Because it already has quite a million degrees.

~ ~ ~

Why couldn't the astronaut focus?
He kept spacing out!

~ ~ ~

HOW DOES A MAN CUT HIS HAIR ON THE MOON?
ECLIPSES IT

~ ~ ~

## Sports Puns

**Why was the baseball player a bad player? He stole third base and then just went home!**

~ ~ ~

I used to wonder why Frisbees looked bigger the closer they came. Then it hit me!

~ ~ ~

Why is a baseball game a good place to go on a hot day?
Because there are lots of fans.

~ ~ ~

I USED TO BE AFRAID OF HURDLES, BUT I GOT OVER IT.

~ ~ ~

I couldn't remember how to throw a boomerang, but it came back to me.

~ ~ ~

Which sport is always in trouble? BADmitton!

~ ~ ~

**My tennis opponent was not happy with my serve. He kept returning it.**

~ ~ ~

Why is tennis such a noisy game?
Because each player raises a racket.

~ ~ ~

WHY DID THE COACH GO TO THE BANK?
TO GET HIS QUARTERBACK.

~ ~ ~

*I wondered if the baseball was getting bigger,
then it hit me.*

~ ~ ~

There's nothing punny about a blank page.

## Puns Around the House

Whenever I undress in the bathroom, my shower gets turned on!

~ ~ ~

Someone stole all my lamps! I couldn't be more de-lighted!

~ ~ ~

WHAT IS THE QUICKEST WAY TO MAKE ANTIFREEZE?
STEAL HER BLANKET!

~ ~ ~

I've started sleeping in our fireplace. Now I sleep like a log!

~ ~ ~

*Towels can't tell a joke. They have a dry sense of humor.*

~ ~ ~

TO WRITE WITH A BROKEN PENCIL IS POINTLESS.

~ ~ ~

What should you do if you're cold? Stand in the corner. It's 90 degrees.

~ ~ ~

*The first computer dates back to Adam and Eve. It was an Apple with limited memory – just one byte. And then everything crashed.*

~ ~ ~

I tried to look up lighters on eBay, but all they had was 13,943 matches.

~ ~ ~

RIP Boiling water. You will be mist.

~ ~ ~

# I used to be addicted to soap, but I'm clean now.

~ ~ ~

Why couldn't the bike stand up on its own?
It was two tired.

~ ~ ~

Cleaning mirrors is a job I could really see myself doing.

~ ~ ~

Did you hear about the new reversible jackets?
I'm excited to see how they turn out.

~ ~ ~

I decided to sell my vacuum cleaner. After all, it was just collecting dust.

~ ~ ~

When is a door not a door?
When it is ajar.

~ ~ ~

I USED TO BUILD STAIRS FOR A LIVING. IT WAS AN UP AND DOWN BUSINESS.

~ ~ ~

Why did the picture end up in jail?
It was framed.

~ ~ ~

*Fixing broken windows is a pane in the glass.*

~ ~ ~

I bought my son a fridge for Christmas. I can't wait to see his face light up when he opens it!

~ ~ ~

**How do you make a Kleenex dance? Put a little boogie in it!**

~ ~ ~

How does a cup steel from you?
He mugs you.

~ ~ ~

**Why did the belt get arrested?
Because it held up a pair of pants.**

~ ~ ~

Want to hear a joke about a piece of paper?
Never mind. It's tearable.

~ ~ ~

I once couldn't afford my electric bill. It was the darkest time of my life.

~ ~ ~

I should have been sad when my flashlight batteries died, but I was delighted.

~ ~ ~

Someone threw a bottle of Omega 3 pills at me! Luckily, my injuries were only super fish oil.

~ ~ ~

## Pun with Dates and Time

DID YOU HEAR ABOUT THE GUY THAT WAS FIRED FROM THE CALENDAR FACTORY? ALL HE DID WAS TAKE A DAY OFF!

~ ~ ~

What does the clock do when it's hungry?
It goes back for seconds!

**Last time I got caught stealing a calendar, I got 12 months.**

~ ~ ~

What time did the man go to the dentist?
Tooth hurt-y!

~ ~ ~

What happened when the semicolon broke grammar laws?
It was given two consecutive sentences.

~ ~ ~

**Sundays are always a little sad, but the day before is a sadder day.**

~ ~ ~

## Language Puns

The past, the present, and the future walked into a bar. It was tense!

~ ~ ~

CAN FEBRUARY MARCH? NO, BUT APRIL MAY!

~ ~ ~

Thanks for explaining the word "many" to me. It means a lot!

~ ~ ~

**Don't spell part backwards. It's a trap!**

~ ~ ~

I bought a dictionary and when I got home, I realized all the pages were blank; I have no words for how angry I am.

~ ~ ~

A huge "thank you" to the person that just explained the word "many" to me. It means a lot.

~ ~ ~

I'm only familiar with 25 letters in the English language. I don't know why.

~ ~ ~

## Puns Like No Others
## (Miscellaneous)

*How did the picture end up in jail?*
*It was framed!*

~ ~ ~

What did one lung say to the other?
We be-lung together!

~ ~ ~

**Sure, I drink brake fluid, but I can stop anytime!**

~ ~ ~

To egotists started a fight. I was an I for an I!

~ ~ ~

I'M GLAD I KNOW SIGN LANGUAGE. IT COMES IN PRETTY HANDY!

~ ~ ~

I wanted to take a picture of fog this morning but mist my chance. I guess I could dew it tomorrow!

~ ~ ~

I saw an ad for a burial plot. That's the last thing I need!

~ ~ ~

I went to a smoke shop to only discover it had been replaced by an apparel store. It was clothes, but no cigar.

~ ~ ~

**What kind of music are balloons afraid of? Pop Music!**

~ ~ ~

What did the left eye say to the right eye?
Between you and me, something smells!

~ ~ ~

Atheism is a non-prophet organization

~ ~ ~

I wasn't going to get a brain transplant, but then I changed my mind.

~ ~ ~

How did I escape Iraq?
Iran.

~ ~ ~

What do you call the security outside of a Samsung Store? Guardians of the Galaxy.

~ ~ ~

I just burned 2,000 calories. That's the last time I leave brownies in the oven while I nap.

~ ~ ~

What's the difference between a poorly dressed man on a bicycle and a nicely dressed man on a tricycle?
A tire!

~ ~ ~

*Confucius say, man who runs behind car will get exhausted, but man who runs in front of car will get tired.*

~ ~ ~

**With great reflexes comes great response ability.**

~ ~ ~

I tried to sue the airline for misplacing my luggage. I lost my case.

~ ~ ~

*The best time to open a gift is the present.*

~ ~ ~

WHAT DID ONE OCEAN SAY TO THE OTHER OCEAN?
NOTHING, THEY JUST WAVED.

~ ~ ~

I'm reading a horror story in Braille. I feel that something is about to happen.

~ ~ ~

*What if there were no hypothetical questions?*

~ ~ ~

**In democracy, it's your vote that counts. In feudalism, it's your count that votes.**

~ ~ ~

A plateau is the highest form of flattery.

~ ~ ~

If the right side of the brain controls the left side of the body, then lefties are the only ones in their right mind.

~ ~ ~

*What do you get when you cross a joke with a rhetorical question?*

~ ~ ~

WILL GLASS COFFINS BE A SUCCESS?
IT REMAINS TO BE SEEN.

~ ~ ~

I made a graph of my past relationships. It has an ex axis and a why axis.

~ ~ ~

Where do sick boats go to get healthy?
To the dock!

~ ~ ~

*I have a phobia of over-engineered buildings. It's a complex complex complex.*

~ ~ ~

The artist thought his favorite paint had been stolen, but it was just a pigment of his imagination.

~ ~ ~

Why was the tree excited about the future?
It was ready to turn over a new leaf!

~ ~ ~

**I got a job in a health club, but they said I wasn't fit for the job.**

~ ~ ~

*I would give my right arm to be ambidextrous!*

~ ~ ~

I always wanted to learn to procrastinate, but I never got around to it.

~ ~ ~

**WHY CAN'T A BANK KEEP A SECRET?
IT HAS TOO MANY TELLERS!**

~ ~ ~

I tried to make a car without wheels. I've been working on it tirelessly.

~ ~ ~

I went to the sign store the other day. I all they had were left-hand turn signs. I didn't buy one because I knew it just wouldn't be right.

~ ~ ~

# I used to be a fan of evolution. But then I evolved.

~ ~ ~

I wanted to bid at a silent auction, but it was not aloud.

~ ~ ~

My friend keeps saying, "Cheer up, it could be worse. You could be stuck underground in a hole full of water." I know he means well.

~ ~ ~

*Spring is here! I was so excited I wet my plants!*

~ ~ ~

A life in politics is full of parties.

~ ~ ~

Did you hear about the circus fire?
It was in tents!

~ ~ ~

**Why didn't the scarecrow win an award?**

**Because he was outstanding in his field.**

~ ~ ~

What do you find in an empty nose?
Fingerprints!

~ ~ ~

I USED TO HATE FACIAL HAIR, BUT THEN IT GREW ON ME.

~ ~ ~

Why are elevator jokes so classic and good?
They work on many levels.

~ ~ ~

**How can you tell it's a dogwood tree? From its bark!**

~ ~ ~

What did Tennessee?
The same thing as Arkansas.

~ ~ ~

**Why was the color green notoriously single? It was always so jaded.**

~ ~ ~

It takes guts to be an organ donor.

~ ~ ~

I LOST MY JOB AT THE BANK ON MY FIRST DAY. A WOMAN ASKED ME TO CHECK HER BALANCE, SO I PUSHED HER OVER.

~ ~ ~

Why is a traffic light red?
You would be red too if you were changing in front of people all day.

~ ~ ~

*Why was the broom late?*
*It over swept.*

~ ~ ~

*I was fired from the candle factory because I refused to work wick ends.*

~ ~ ~

I started a company selling landmines that look like prayer mats. Prophets are going through the roof!

~ ~ ~

**My friend is in prison for flashing.
He says he can't bare it anymore.**

~ ~ ~

What kind of shorts to clouds wear? Thunderwear!

~ ~ ~

I was addicted to the hokey pokey...
but thankfully, I turned myself around.

~ ~ ~

A TICKET FOR SPEEDING IS FINE
WITH ME....

~ ~ ~

For fungi to grow, you must
give it as mushroom as possible.

~ ~ ~

An expensive laxative will give you a
run for your money.

~ ~ ~

# I couldn't figure out how to put my seatbelt on, but then it clicked!

~ ~ ~

*I don't think I need a spine. It is holding me back.*

~ ~ ~

I recently took a pole and found that 100% of the occupants were angry with me when their tent collapsed.

~ ~ ~

MY JOB AT THE CONCRETE PLANT SEEMED TO GET HARDER AND HARDER.

~ ~ ~

Did you know they won't be making yard sticks any longer?

~ ~ ~

At first I was intimidated by punning, but it's groan on me.

~ ~ ~

This book was published by Yowza Publishing

Check out our complete line of books at:

YowzaPublishing.com

www.ingramcontent.com/pod-product-compliance
Lightning Source LLC
Chambersburg PA
CBHW071518040426
42444CB00008B/1695